Zola Discovers

SOUTH AFRICA

by Alexandria Pereira

AuthorHouse™
1663 Liberty Drive
Bloomington, IN 47403
www.authorhouse.com
Phone: 833-262-8899

Because of the dynamic nature of the Internet, any web addresses or links contained in this book may have changed since publication and may no longer be valid. The views expressed in this work are solely those of the author and do not necessarily reflect the views of the publisher, and the publisher hereby disclaims any responsibility for them.

This book is printed on acid-free paper.

ISBN: 978-1-6655-5358-2 (sc)
ISBN: 978-1-6655-5359-9 (hc)
ISBN: 978-1-6655-5360-5 (e)

Library of Congress Control Number: 2022903981

Print information available on the last page.

Published by AuthorHouse 03/10/2022

authorHOUSE®

The Mystery of History Series
South Africa
Book 1 of 4

Dedication

To my grandma – whose life work was dedicated to
children and their pursuit of knowledge.

"Grandma, where do I come from," asked Zola.

"I am so glad you asked Zola. You know that you are part of a family. Your mother is my child, and my mother is your great grandmother. She had a mother too. These are our ancestors, the people that came before you. Zola, you are part of a family," said Grandma.

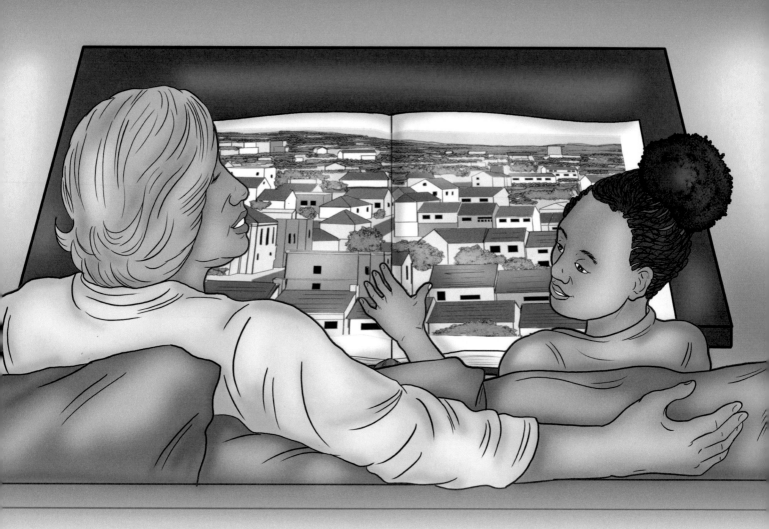

"But where do I come from? It is a mystery to me," asked Zola.

"Well, our family is also part of a bigger family. All the people who live in our city are part of our city family - our neighbors, the people at your school, even the people that work in the stores.

"There are other cities with families who live in them too.
Let's take a look!

This is the City of Cape Town.
This is the City of Tulbagh.
And this is the City of Johannesburg.

All these cities make up an even bigger family.

"We call this even bigger family a country. Our country is called South Africa. It sits at the bottom of the Continent of Africa. Let's hop in my car and discover some more.

"South Africa has deserts. One of the biggest deserts is the Kalahari Desert. It is so big it is shared with the Countries of South Africa, Namibia and Botswana on the Continent of Africa.

"South Africa has mountains, like Drakensberg. Most of the water for South Africa comes from the snow when it melts off of the top of the Drakensberg Mountains.

"There is even a whole other country inside the Drakensberg Mountains of South Africa. It is called Lesotho. Lesotho has its own king.

"South Africa has rivers, like the Orange River. It is the longest river in South Africa, but no boats can sail on it because it is not deep enough.

"South Africa has plateaus. Plateaus are flat open areas, lying high between big mountain ranges. Some plateaus are covered with grass and some are dotted with trees.

"And on those grass and tree plateaus, live the animals of South Africa.
Lions, elephants, and giraffes roam the plateaus looking for food, or lay down and just take a nap.

"South Africa has small animals too, like vervet monkeys, baboons and seals that play near the ocean, while many kinds of birds fly around overhead.

"South Africa has three different kinds of forests.

There are very wet forests, called wetlands, with lakes and swamps, and a lot of birds.

There are forests that are a little wet, called subtropical, that stay hot or warm all year long.

"And there are drier forests called woodland or bushland. The San people live on the bushland and still hunt and gather for their food.

"South Africa has beaches, were sometimes penguins play. Look out to sea, you might see great white sharks and dolphins swimming after sardines in June.

"South Africa has a lot of farmland; were they grow all kinds of food to eat and drink.

"And South Africa has people, a lot of people. Their ancestors came from so many different countries. But all of them call South Africa home.

They speak different languages - English, Afrikaans, isiZulu, isiXhosa, IsiNdebele, Sesotho, Northern Sotho, Setswana, siSwati, Tshivenda, and Xitsonga.

They enjoy different cultures and customs - Zulu, Xhosa, Pedi, Tswana, Ndebele, Khoisan, Hindu, Muslim, Afrikaner and others.

They have many different ways to say "Hello: Heita, Sawubona, Aweh, and Dumela," say "How are you: Hoe gaan dit, Howzit, Thobela, Unjani, and Molo?" and say "Hello and how are you: Sharp Fede?"

South Africa calls itself the Rainbow Nation, because so many beautiful colorful people are part of its bigger family," said Grandma.

"Here I am with my grandma. I see how all the cities, mountains, rivers, plateaus, animals, forests, beaches, farmland, and people are part of my bigger family. I come from this big family, the Country of South Africa. My history is no longer a mystery.

Thank you, Grandma," said Zola.

"You are welcome," said Grandma.

Educational Support Activities

Explain to understand – Basic Human Needs
We need food to grow, clothing to keep us warm, and shelter to keep us safe and dry.
We need to socialize to work together.
We need to solve problems so we can invent and be creative.

Practical Life and Sensorial Foundation
Plant a seed. Go on a berry hunt. Why do these things?

History
Use a timeline to show and ask what happened: past, present, and future.

Science
Build a model of a mud and grass hut.
Paint rocks using crushed charcoal and pigments, like berries; use twigs for brushes.

Geography and Map Work
Find the Continent of Africa on a map. Find South Africa on the African Continent.
Trace South Africa and draw significant landforms, mountains, rivers, plateaus, beaches.

Language
Make up a new primitive language using signs or clicks. What are you saying?

Botany
What products do South African's grow? Peel an orange, eat a bunch of grapes, a pear.

Printed in the United States
by Baker & Taylor Publisher Services